THE OFFICIAL CRYSTAL PALACE ANNUAL 2025

A Grange Publication

Author: Andrew McSteen   Designed by: Chris Dalrymple

© 2024. Published by Grange Communications Ltd., Edinburgh, under licence from Crystal Palace Football Club. Printed in the EU.

Every effort has been made to ensure the accuracy of information within this publication, but the publishers cannot be held responsible for any errors or omissions. Every effort has been made to identify copyright holders and obtain their permission for the use of copyright material. Views expressed are those of the author and do not necessarily represent those of the publishers or the football club. All rights reserved.

Photo Credits: Sebastian Frej (Crystal Palace FC), Neil Everitt, Chris Smith (Brickstand), Pinnacle Photo Agency Ltd (PPAUK), Getty Images, Sunsplash Productions

Thanks: Foz Bowers, Robin Johnson, Will Robinson, Toby Jagmohan, Matt Franks, Terry Byfield, Sammy Brough, Sebastian Frej (Crystal Palace FC), Shannon McLoughlan (Crystal Palace FC Women), Tommy Macarthur (Palace for Life Foundation), Chris Smith (Brickstand), Christopher Sleet (Getty Images), Philip Mingo (Pinnacle Photo Agency Ltd), Dan Weir (Crystal Pix/PPAUK), Phil Morgan (PNM Design @pnm1979), Alice Burdett-Coutts (Grange Communications), Rebecca Lowe (NBC), Neil Everitt, Ian King, Roy Peskett ('The Crystal Palace Story'), Karen Amaradivakara, Steve Martyniuk.

ISBN: 978-1-915879-81-3

CONTENTS

- **6** CLUB INFORMATION AND HONOURS
- **7** 2024/25: KITS
- **8-9** 2024/25: MEN'S OPPONENTS
- **11-13** PALACE MEN'S SQUAD 2024/25
- **14** POSTER: GOALKEEPERS
- **15** POSTER: DEFENDERS
- **16-17** PALACE WOMEN'S SQUAD 2024/25
- **18-26** 2023/24: MEN'S SEASON REVIEW
- **28-29** 2023/24: WOMEN'S SEASON REVIEW
- **30-31** 2023/24: WOMEN – CHAMPIONS
- **32** POSTER: MIDFIELDERS
- **33** THE ACADEMY
- **34-35** 2023/24: PREMIER LEAGUE INTERNATIONAL CUP CHAMPIONS
- **36** 2023/24: RECORD BREAKERS/MILESTONES

THE OFFICIAL 2024/25 CRYSTAL PALACE KITS

The Macron home kit is a return to the club's trademark red and blue stripes, with embedded repeated eagles nesting within the contrasting sections and a fine red, white and blue trim sported around the collar and sleeves, with matching shorts.

As part of the club's celebrations to mark 100 years since the official opening of Selhurst Park, the kit also features a commemorative 'stamp' on the back collar of the shirt.

The kit is completed by blue shorts that also feature a repeating eagles pattern, as well as side splashes of red, and blue socks with thin lines in red and white around the fold.

Eagle Yellow is the first Palace strip to feature a simplified eagle-on-ball crest, replacing the standard crest to highlight this iconic symbol of South London.

The strip also features an embedded eagle within a striking yellow-and-blue design, with matching shorts and socks. Eagle Yellow follows in a long tradition of yellow kits for the club over the years, with the colour first emerging in the 1960s. The design also features blue on the hems, with additional fine red stripes on the collar.

Finally, there's Eagle Black, which layers the famous red and blue stripes of our Home Kit upon on a black background of embossed, faded Eagle motifs. The striking strip also features asymmetrical red and blue stripes on either sleeve and leg of the shorts, with collar and hems also adorned by Palace's famous colours.

As in previous seasons, the Macron kit has sustainability at its heart and is made from Eco Fabric, a polyester material 100% derived from recycled plastic and certified by the Global Recycled Standard.

The shirt is made from Eco Sirena Light with eco micromesh in the back for reduced weight and improved breathability, whilst the shorts are made from Eco Softlock and Eco mesh.

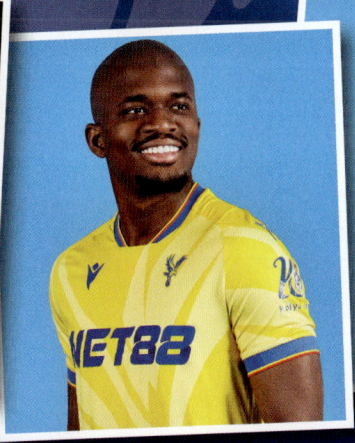

2024/25 MEN'S OPPONENTS

ARSENAL
Established: 1886
Nickname: The Gunners
Ground: Emirates Stadium
Capacity: 60,704
Built: 2006
Pitch size: 105m x 68m
Last Season: 2nd
Premier League Head-to-Head: Played 30 Won 4 Drawn 8 Lost 18

ASTON VILLA
Established: 1874
Nickname: The Villans
Ground: Villa Park
Capacity: 42,530
Opened: 1897
Pitch size: 105m x 68m
Last Season: 4th
Premier League Head-to-Head: Played 24 Won 9 Drawn 6 Lost 9

BOURNEMOUTH
Established: 1899
Nickname: The Cherries
Ground: Vitality Stadium
Capacity: 11,307
Built: 1910
Pitch size: 105m x 68m
Last Season: 12th
Premier League Head-to-Head vs Palace: Played 14 Won 6 Drawn 4 Lost 4

BRENTFORD
Established: 1889
Nickname: The Bees
Ground: Brentford Community Stadium
Capacity: 17,250
Built: 2020
Pitch size: 105m x 68m
Last Season: 16th
Premier League Head-to-Head: Played 6 Won 1 Drawn 5 Lost 0

BRIGHTON AND HOVE ALBION
Established: 1901
Nickname: The Seagulls
Ground: Amex Stadium
Capacity: 31,876
Built: 2011
Pitch size: 105m x 68m
Last Season: 11th
Premier League Head-to-Head: Played 14 Won 3 Drawn 7 Lost 4

CHELSEA
Established: 1905
Nickname: The Blues
Ground: Stamford Bridge
Capacity: 40,343
Built: 1877
Pitch size: 103m x 67.5m
Last Season: 6th
Premier League Head-to-Head: Played 30 Won 4 Drawn 2 Lost 24

EVERTON
Established: 1878
Nickname: The Toffees
Ground: Goodison Park
Capacity: 39,414
Built: 1892
Pitch size: 100.48m x 68m
Last Season: 15th
Premier League Head-to-Head: Played 30 Won 6 Drawn 10 Lost 14

FULHAM
Established: 1879
Nickname: The Cottagers
Ground: Craven Cottage
Capacity: 22,384
Opened: 1896
Pitch size: 100m x 65m
Last Season: 13th
Premier League Head-to-Head: Played 12 Won 4 Drawn 5 Lost 3

IPSWICH TOWN
Established: 1878
Nickname: The Tractor Boys
Ground: Portman Road
Capacity: 29,763
Opened: 1884
Pitch size: 102m x 75m
Last Season: Promoted from Championship
Premier League Head-to-Head: Played 4 Won 1 Drawn 3 Lost 0

LEICESTER CITY
Established: 1884
Nickname: The Foxes
Ground: King Power Stadium
Capacity: 32,262
Opened: 2002
Pitch size: 105m x 68m
Last Season: Promoted from Championship
Premier League Head-to-Head: Played 22 Won 9 Drawn 5 Lost 8

LIVERPOOL
Established: 1892
Nickname: The Reds
Ground: Anfield
Capacity: 61,276
Built: 1884 (redeveloped 1928, 2016)
Pitch size: 101m x 68m
Last Season: 3rd
Premier League Head-to-Head: Played 30 Won 6 Drawn 5 Lost 19

MAN CITY
Established: 1887
Nickname: The Citizens
Ground: Etihad Stadium
Capacity: 53,400 **Built:** 2002
Pitch size: 105m x 68m
Last Season: 1st/Champions
Premier League Head-to-Head: Played 26 Won 4 Drawn 6 Lost 16

MAN UNITED
Established: 1878
Nickname: Red Devils
Ground: Old Trafford
Capacity: 74,310 **Built:** 1909
Pitch size: 105m x 68m
Last Season: 8th
Premier League Head-to-Head: Played 30 Won 5 Drawn 6 Lost 19

NEWCASTLE UNITED
Established: 1892
Nickname: The Magpies
Ground: St. James' Park
Capacity: 52,305
Built: 1892 (expanded 2000)
Pitch size: 105m x 68m
Last Season: 7th
Premier League Head-to-Head: Played 26 Won 6 Drawn 8 Lost 12

NOTTINGHAM FOREST
Established: 1865
Nickname: Forest
Ground: The City Ground
Capacity: 30,404 **Opened:** 1898
Pitch size: 102m x 68m
Last Season: 17th
Premier League Head-to-Head: Played 8 Won 0 Drawn 5 Lost 3

SOUTHAMPTON
Established: 1885
Nickname: The Saints
Ground: St. Mary's
Capacity: 32,384 **Opened:** 2001
Pitch size: 105m x 68m
Last Season: Promoted from Championship
Premier League Head-to-Head: Played 28 Won 7 Drawn 7 Lost 14

TOTTENHAM HOTSPUR
Established: 1882
Nickname: Spurs
Ground: Tottenham Hotspur Stadium **Capacity:** 62,850
Built: 2019
Pitch size: 105m x 68m
Last Season: 5th
Premier League Head-to-Head: Played 30 Won 4 Drawn 7 Lost 19

WEST HAM UNITED
Established: 1895
Nickname: The Hammers
Ground: London Stadium
Capacity: 62,500 **Built:** 2011
Pitch size: 105m x 68m
Last Season: 9th
Premier League Head-to-Head: Played 26 Won 9 Drawn 8 Lost 9

WOLVERHAMPTON WANDERERS
Established: 1877
Nickname: Wolves
Ground: Molineux Stadium
Capacity: 31,750 **Built:** 1889
Pitch size: 105m x 68m
Last Season: 14th
Premier League Head-to-Head: Played 12 Won 7 Drawn 1 Lost 4

*All data correct at time of print

STADIUM TOURS

1924 SELHURST PARK 2024

EXPERIENCE SELHURST PARK LIKE NEVER BEFORE

GO BEHIND THE SCENES
MEDIA CENTRE / CHANGING ROOM / TEAM DUGOUTS / WALKOUT TUNNEL

SEARCH 'CPFC STADIUM TOUR'

PALACE MEN'S SQUAD 2024/25

GOALKEEPERS

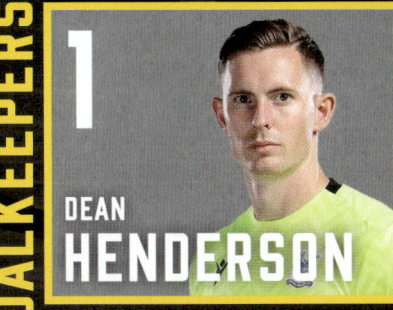

1 DEAN HENDERSON
Country: England
Date of Birth: 12/03/1997
Signed: 31/08/2023
Instagram: @deanhenderson

30 MATT TURNER
Country: USA
Date of Birth: 24/06/1994
Signed: 30/08/2024
Instagram: @headdturnerr

31 REMI MATTHEWS
Country: England
Date of Birth: 10/02/1994
Signed: 13/07/2021
Instagram: @remimatthews

DEFENDERS

2 JOEL WARD
Country: England
Date of Birth: 29/10/1989
Signed: 29/05/2012
Instagram: @JoelWard2

3 TYRICK MITCHELL
Country: England
Date of Birth: 01/09/1999
Signed: 01/06/2016
Instagram: @TMitch.27

4 ROB HOLDING
Country: England
Date of Birth: 20/09/1995
Signed: 01/09/2023
Instagram: @rholding95

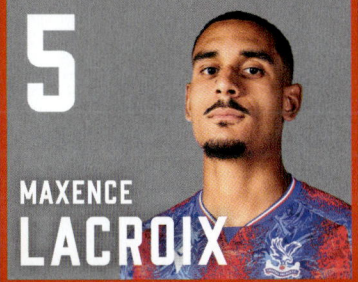

5 MAXENCE LACROIX
Country: France
Date of Birth: 06/04/2000
Signed: 30/08/2024
Instagram: @lacroix_maxence

6 MARC GUÉHI
Country: England
Date of Birth: 13/07/2000
Signed: 18/07/2021

12 DANIEL MUÑOZ
Country: Colombia
Date of Birth: 26/05/1996
Signed: 30/01/2024
Instagram: @daniel.chitiva

SQUAD 2024/25

17 NATHANIEL CLYNE
Country: England
Date of Birth: 05/04/1991
Signed: 14/10/2020
Instagram: @Nathaniel_Clyne

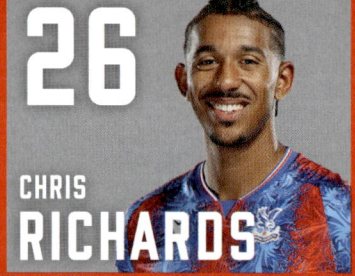

26 CHRIS RICHARDS
Country: USA
Date of Birth: 28/03/2000
Signed: 27/07/2022
Instagram: @eastmamba

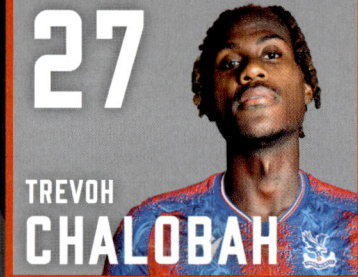

27 TREVOH CHALOBAH
Country: England
Date of Birth: 05/07/1999
Signed: 30/08/2024
Instagram: @yungchalobah

34 CHADI RIAD
Country: Morocco
Date of Birth: 17/06/2003
Signed: 02/07/2024
Instagram: @chadiriad17

MIDFIELDERS

8 JEFFERSON LERMA
Country: Colombia
Date of Birth: 25/10/1994
Signed: 01/07/2023
Instagram: @jeffersonlerma

10 EBERE EZE
Country: England
Date of Birth: 29/06/1998
Signed: 28/08/2020
Instagram: @Ebere10

15 JEFFREY SCHLUPP
Country: Ghana
Date of Birth: 23/12/1992
Signed: 13/01/2017
Instagram: @JeffreySchlupp

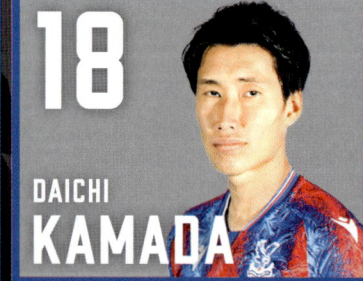

18 DAICHI KAMADA
Country: Japan
Date of Birth: 05/08/1996
Signed: 01/07/2024
Instagram: @kamadadaichi

SQUAD 2024/25

19 WILL HUGHES
Country: England
Date of Birth: 17/04/1995
Signed: 28/08/2021
Instagram: @wjhughes19

20 ADAM WHARTON
Country: England
Date of Birth: 06/02/2004
Signed: 01/02/2024
Instagram: @adamwharton10

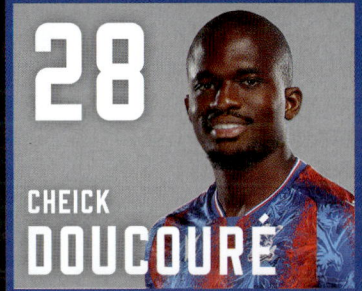

28 CHEICK DOUCOURÉ
Country: Mali
Date of Birth: 08/01/2000
Signed: 11/07/2022
Instagram: @cheick.doucoure20

FORWARDS

7 ISMAÏLA SARR
Country: Senegal
Date of Birth: 11/09/1991
Signed: 01/08/2024
Instagram: @ismaila_sarr_18

9 EDDIE NKETIAH
Country: England
Date of Birth: 30/05/1999
Signed: 30/08/2024
Instagram: @eddienketiah

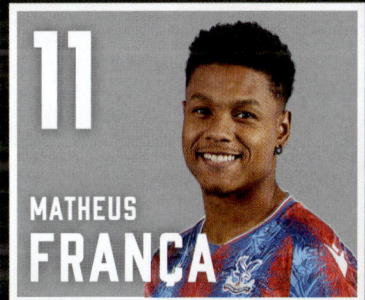

11 MATHEUS FRANÇA
Country: Brazil
Date of Birth: 01/04/2004
Signed: 05/08/2023
Instagram: @matheus_franca04

14 JEAN-PHILIPPE MATETA
Country: France
Date of Birth: 28/06/1997
Signed: 21/01/2021
Instagram: @IAmMateta

*all squad details correct at time of print

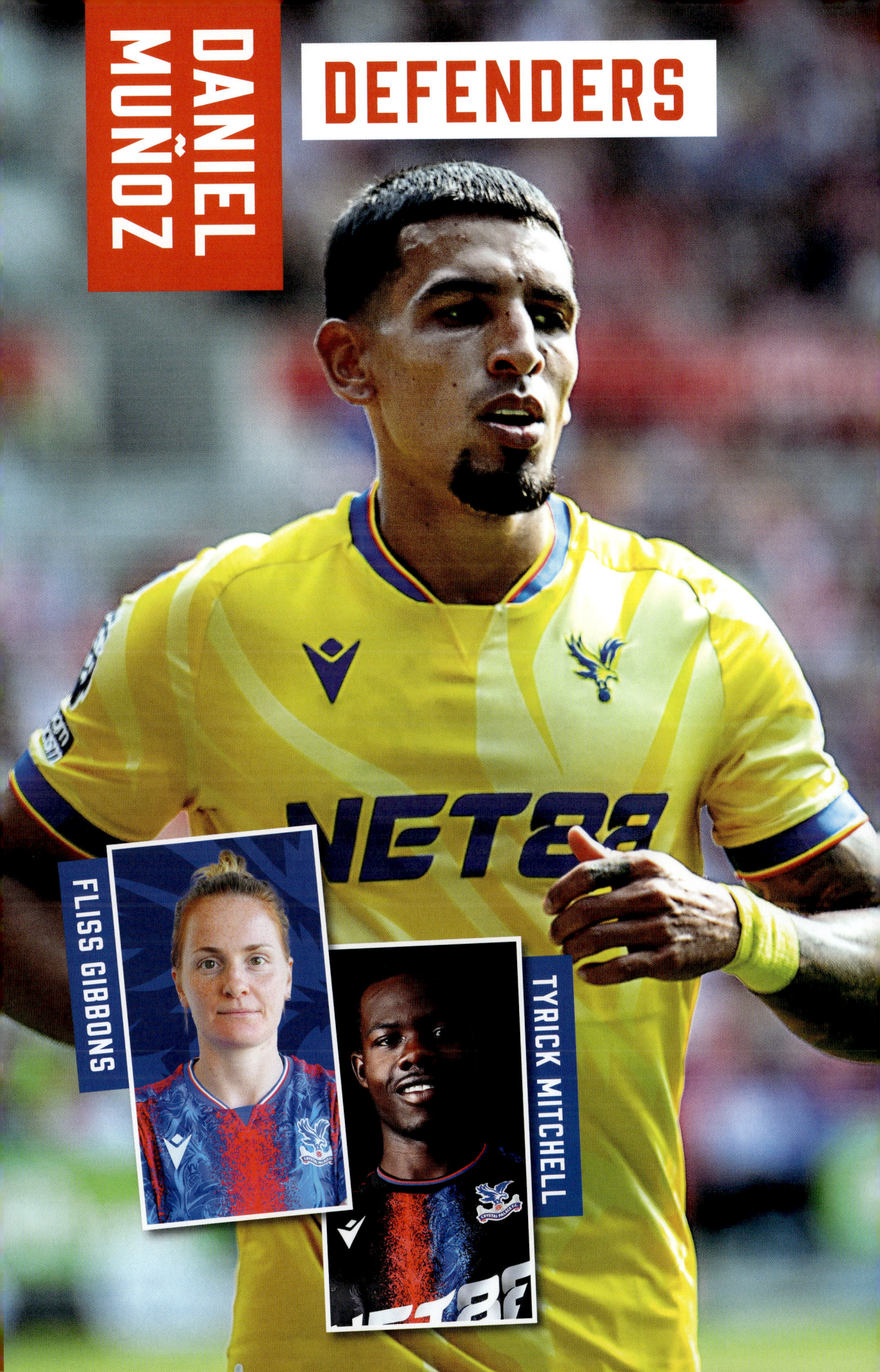

PALACE WOMEN'S SQUAD 2024/25

GOALKEEPERS

19 MILLA-MAJ MAJASAARI
Country: Finland
Date of Birth: 15/10/1999
Signed: 31/08/2024
Instagram: @millamajasaari

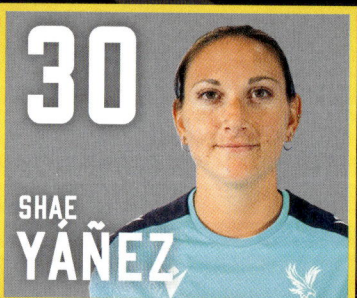

30 SHAE YÁÑEZ
Country: USA
Date of Birth: 22/05/1997
Signed: 02/08/2024
Instagram: @shaeyanez

31 ANNIS-CLARA WRIGHT
Country: England
Date of Birth: 25/03/2007
Signed: Academy
Instagram: @acw.14

DEFENDERS

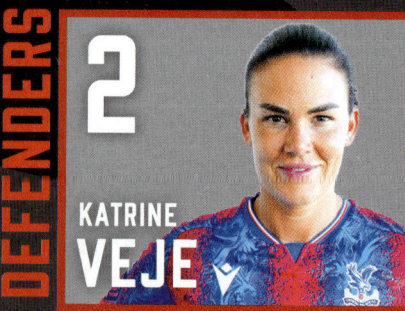

2 KATRINE VEJE
Country: Denmark
Date of Birth: 19/06/1991
Signed: 01/08/2024
Instagram: @katrinevejsgaardveje

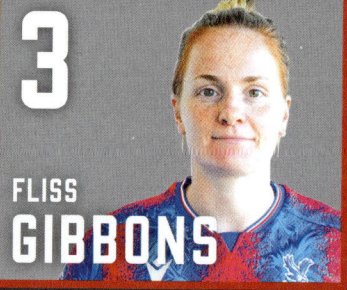

3 FLISS GIBBONS
Country: England
Date of Birth: 09/07/1994
Signed: 01/07/2022

4 CHLOE ARTHUR
Country: Scotland
Date of Birth: 21/01/1995
Signed: 01/07/2022
Instagram: @chloearthur77

6 AIMEE EVERETT
Country: England
Date of Birth: 02/08/2001
Signed: 01/07/2021
Instagram: @aimee.everett

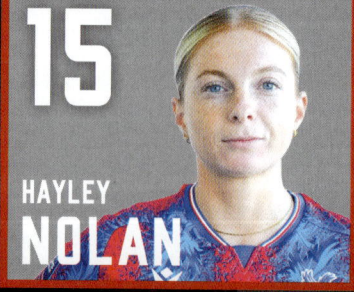

15 HAYLEY NOLAN
Country: Ireland
Date of Birth: 07/03/1997
Signed: 01/07/2023
Instagram: @Hayley__Nolan

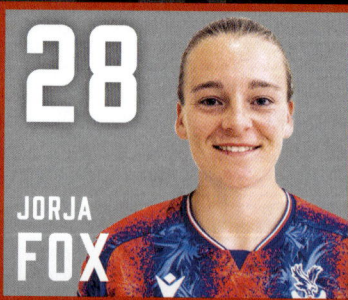

28 JORJA FOX
Country: England
Date of Birth: 28/08/2003
Signed: 15/08/2024
Instagram: @jorjafox

MIDFIELDERS

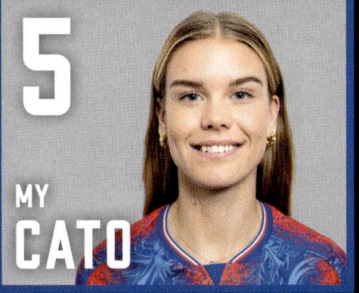

5 MY CATO
Country: Sweden
Date of Birth: 25/04/2002
Signed: 01/09/2024
Instagram: @mycatoo

14 JOSIE GREEN
Country: Wales
Date of Birth: 25/04/1993
Signed: 31/08/2024
Instagram: @josiexgreen

17 LEXI POTTER
Country: England
Date of Birth: 17/08/2006
Signed: 31/08/2024
Instagram: @lexi.potter

21 MILLE GEJL
Country: Denmark
Date of Birth: 23/09/1999
Signed: 15/08/24
Instagram: @millegejljensen

24 SHANADE HOPCROFT
Country: England
Date of Birth: 04/10/1997
Signed: 01/07/2023
Instagram: @shanadehopcroft

FORWARDS

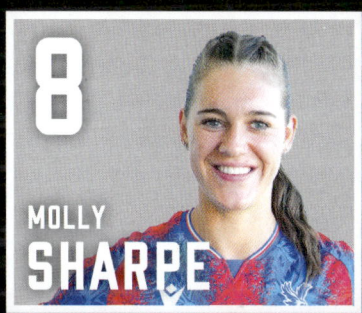

8 MOLLY SHARPE
Country: England
Date of Birth: 12/03/1998
Signed: 01/07/2021
Instagram: @mollysharpe_

9 ELISE HUGHES
Country: Wales
Date of Birth: 15/04/2001
Signed: 01/07/2022
Instagram: @elise__hughes

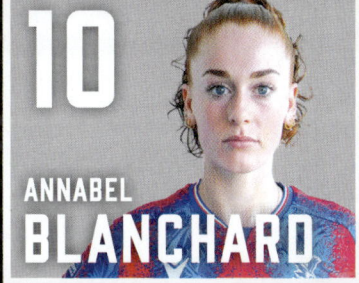

10 ANNABEL BLANCHARD
Country: England
Date of Birth: 07/05/2001
Signed: 01/07/2022
Instagram: @annabelblanchard

11 ASHLEIGH WEERDEN
Country: Netherlands
Date of Birth: 07/06/1999
Signed: 08/08/2024
Instagram: @ashweerden

20 INDIAH-PAIGE RILEY
Country: New Zealand
Date of Birth: 20/12/2001
Signed: 07/08/2024
Instagram: @indiahriley

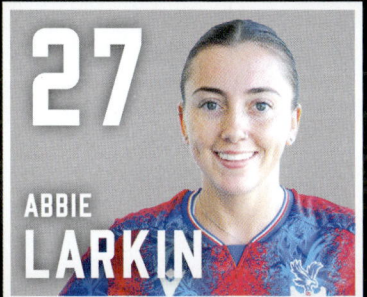

27 ABBIE LARKIN
Country: Ireland
Date of Birth: 27/04/2005
Signed: 31/01/2024
Instagram: @abbielarkinn

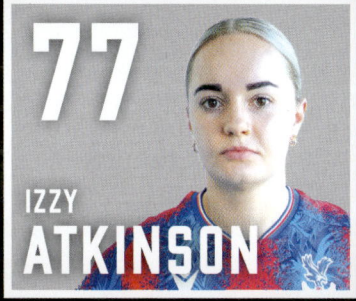

77 IZZY ATKINSON
Country: Ireland
Date of Birth: 17/07/2001
Signed: 27/01/2024
Instagram: @izzy_atkinson_

*all squad details correct at time of print

MEN'S SEASON REVIEW 2023/24

Ahead of the new season, the Eagles faced Barnet (0-1), Brøndby IF (2-2), Crawley (4-0), Watford (2-1), Millonarios (1-2), Sevilla (1-1) and Lyon (2-0) in pre-season.

PREMIER LEAGUE

SHEFFIELD UNITED 0-1 PALACE
Édouard 49

12/08/23: A sunny start to the new campaign saw Jefferson Lerma make his Palace debut in midfield as Odsonne Édouard's early second half strike gained all three points.

BRENTFORD 1-1 PALACE
Schade 18
Andersen 76

26/08/23: After going down early on, the Eagles rallied and were rewarded with a Joachim Andersen equaliser, which he prodded in past Brentford goalkeeper Mark Flekken.

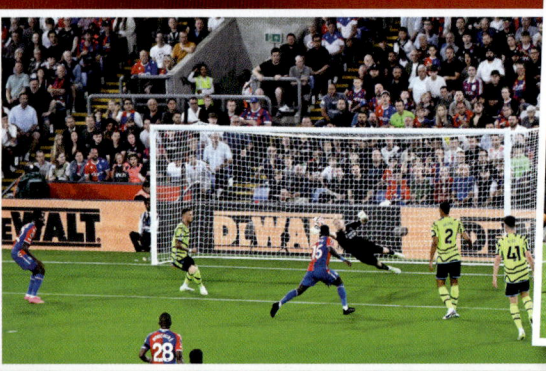

PALACE 0-1 ARSENAL
Ødegaard 54 (p)

21/08/23: Monday Night Football under the lights saw the home side lose to a Martin Ødegaard penalty despite playing against 10 men after Tomiyasu was sent off for the visitors. Jeffrey Schlupp made his 200th appearance for Palace. Ahead of the game there was a minute's applause for former manager Trevor Francis and former Millwall chairman and owner John Berylson who had passed away recently.

PALACE 3-2 WOLVES
Édouard 56, 84, Eze 78
Hee-Chan 65, Cunha 90+

03/09/23: Transfer window signing Dean Henderson appeared as an Eagle for the first time, albeit on the bench, as Roy Hodgson named the same starting line-up for the fourth Premier League game in a row. On the pitch, all five goals were scored in the second half. Édouard again delivered, scoring a brace to put the SE25 outfit 3-1 ahead and on their way to another three points.

ASTON VILLA 3-1 PALACE
Durán 87, Douglas Luiz 90+8, Bailey 90+11
Édouard 47

16/09/23: Despite losing key players Marc Guéhi and Jefferson Lerma to injury on international break and manager Roy Hodgson – who had been taken unwell earlier in the day – leaving managerial duties to Paddy McCarthy, assisted by Ray Lewington – Édouard put the Eagles ahead but a very late rally from Villa grabbed the points.

PALACE 0-0 NOTTINGHAM FOREST

07/10/23: An uneventful game saw Palace withstand late Forest pressure to earn a third consecutive Premier League clean sheet.

PALACE 0-0 FULHAM

23/09/23: Hodgson was back for the match against his former club, but despite their best efforts, his Crystal Palace side could not find their way past the dogged West London outfit.

NEWCASTLE UNITED 4-0 PALACE
Murphy 4, Gordon 44, Longstaff 45+2, Wilson 66

21/10/23: Matheus França made his first appearance in a matchday squad since signing from Flamengo in the summer, but with Newcastle firing on all cylinders, the Eagles' second-best defensive record in the Premier League was wiped out.

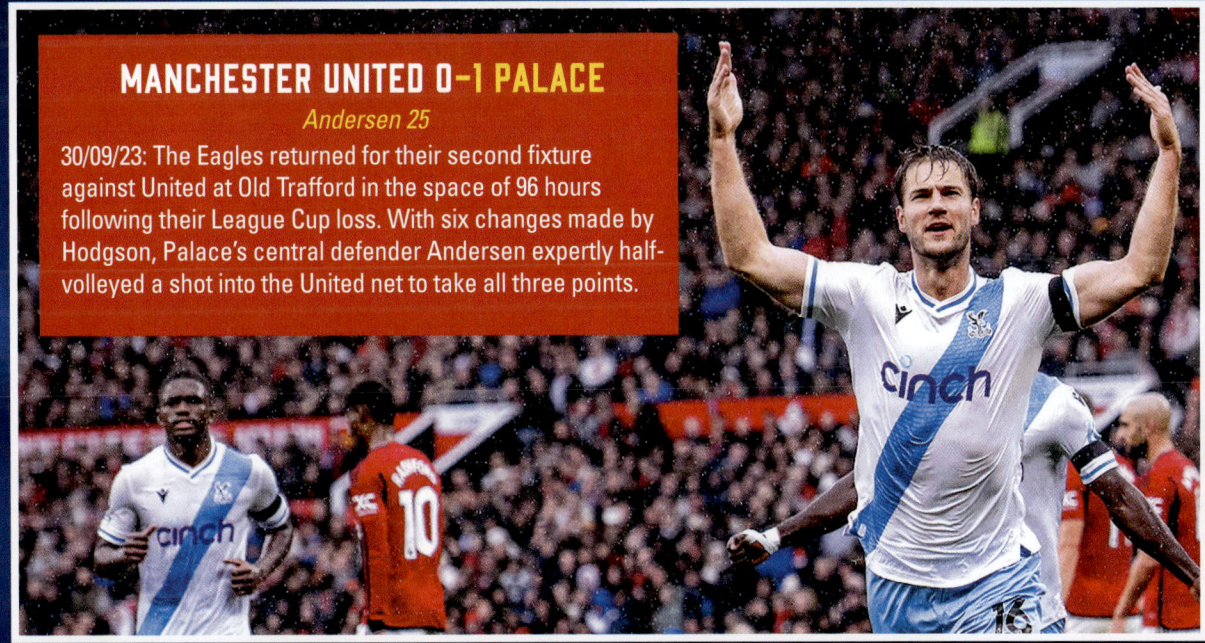

MANCHESTER UNITED 0-1 PALACE
Andersen 25

30/09/23: The Eagles returned for their second fixture against United at Old Trafford in the space of 96 hours following their League Cup loss. With six changes made by Hodgson, Palace's central defender Andersen expertly half-volleyed a shot into the United net to take all three points.

PALACE 1-2 TOTTENHAM HOTSPUR
Ayew 90+4
Ward 53 (og), Son 66

27/10/23: Jordan Ayew's outrageous half-volley in additional time was not enough to claw back a point against the North London side. França made his home Palace debut while Nathaniel Clyne made his 200th senior appearance for the Eagles.

LUTON TOWN 2-1 PALACE
Mengi 72, Brown 83
Olise 74

25/11/23: A goal-of-the-season contender from Olise – the 600th Premier League goal for the Eagles – making his first start of the season, was sandwiched in-between two Luton goals in the last 20 minutes, as both Eze and then Cheick Doucouré suffered long-term injuries.

BURNLEY 0-2 PALACE
Schlupp 22, Mitchell 90+4

04/11/23: Ebere Eze returned from a long injury lay-off and this inspired the Eagles to three points with a goal in either half. Mitchell's late strike was his first goal for Palace since 2021.

WEST HAM UNITED 1-1 PALACE
Kudus 13
Édouard 53

03/12/23: A rejigged Palace side, with Chris Richards in defensive midfield, secured a point thanks to another Édouard strike.

PALACE 2-3 EVERTON
Eze 5, Édouard 74,
Mykolenko 1, Doucouré 49, Gueye 86

11/11/23: On Armistice Day, Eze returned to the starting XI after signing a new contract and Michael Olise appeared on the bench for his first matchday squad appearance following a 139-day injury lay-off. However, an impressive performance from the visitors saw them take the lead three times, with Gueye's late goal proving decisive.

PALACE 0-2 BOURNEMOUTH
Senesi 25, Moore 90+1

06/12/23: Olise started his first game back at Selhurst Park after injury but could not prevent a disappointing day at the office for the SE25 outfit.

PALACE 1-2 LIVERPOOL
Mateta 57 (p)
Salah 76, Elliott 90+1

09/12/23: Joel Ward's 350th appearance for the Eagles saw Mateta come on as second half sub and then win and convert a penalty to put his side 1-0 ahead. But a controversial second yellow card for Ayew, combined with a fortuitous Mohamed Salah goal moments later, transformed the game and Liverpool won it in injury time.

PALACE 1-1 BRIGHTON
Ayew 45+1
Welbeck 82

21/12/23: A delightful, dipping cross from Olise swept onto the head of Ayew inside the six-yard box to put the home side ahead just before the break, but Danny Welbeck's late strike ensured the points were shared.

MANCHESTER CITY 2-2 PALACE
Grealish 24, Lewis 54
Mateta 76, Olise 90+5 (p)

16/12/23: Summer signing Henderson made his first Premier League start for the Eagles after returning from injury, coming in to replace the injured Sam Johnstone. Olise's late equaliser from the spot secured a point against the eventual league champions.

CHELSEA 2-1 PALACE
Mudryk 13, Madueke 89 (p)
Olise 45+1

27/12/23: Eze returned to the Palace first team for the first time since November but the Eagles were undone yet again by a late goal, this time from the penalty spot. Former Chelsea academy player Olise had brought the teams level with an incisive volleyed finish from an Ayew cross.

PALACE 3-1 BRENTFORD
Olise 14, 58, Eze 39
Lewis-Potter 2

30/12/23: The final game of 2023 ended with a bang as fans were treated to the rare sight of both Olise and Eze playing together. The pair caused havoc for Brentford's defence scoring all three goals for the home side in a comprehensive win.

ARSENAL 5-0 PALACE
Gabriel 11, 37, Trossard 59, Martinelli 90+4, 90+5

20/01/24: North London rivals Arsenal completely overpowered the Eagles at the Emirates as Hodgson's side suffered their worst defeat of the season.

PALACE 1-3 CHELSEA
Lerma 30
Gallagher 47, 90+1 Fernández 90+4

12/02/24: In what would prove to be Hodgson's final game in charge of the club, two late goals won it for Chelsea. França and Wharton made their first Premier League starts, joined by Muñoz playing his first game at Selhurst Park. Lerma's spectacular strike was Palace's 1000th top-flight goal and put his side ahead, but former loan player Conor Gallagher came back to haunt his old side, scoring a brace to seal the away win.

PALACE 3-2 SHEFFIELD UNITED
Eze 17, 27, Olise 67
Brereton 1, McAtee 20

30/01/24: An action-packed first-half saw four goals, with the returning-from-injury Olise twice setting up Eze for two brilliant finishes and then scoring the winner later on.

BRIGHTON 4-1 PALACE
Dunk 3, Hinshelwood 33, Buonanotte 34, Pedro 85
Mateta 71

03/02/24: Winter transfer window signings Daniel Muñoz and Adam Wharton made their Palace debuts as rivals Brighton handed the Eagles a comprehensive defeat. To make matters worse, Guéhi suffered an injury which would require an operation and keep him out until the end of the season while Olise came on as a sub only to aggravate his previous injury and leave the field of play moments later.

EVERTON 1-1 PALACE
Onana 84,
Ayew 66

19/02/24: New boss Oliver Glasner was in Merseyside watching on from the stands, as McCarthy and Lewington oversaw a 1-1 draw against Everton. An Ayew thunderbolt fired Palace into a deserved lead, but Onana's header meant the points were split.

A break in Premier League action saw the Eagles travel to Marbella, Spain for a training camp where they played Bodø/Glimt on 14/03/24 and won 1-0 (Eze 23).

PALACE 3-0 BURNLEY
Richards 68, Ayew 71, Mateta 79 (p)

24/02/24: The Glasner era started with a comprehensive 3-0 demolition of Burnley. An unlikely goalscorer opened the Glasner account, when Chris Richards headed home midway through the second half, quickly followed by an Ayew goal and Mateta penalty.

NOTTINGHAM FOREST 1-1 PALACE
Wood 61
Mateta 11

30/03/24: Mateta scored again as the Eagles returned to competitive action after three weeks off, but Wood's speculative header looped over Henderson to share the points.

TOTTENHAM HOTSPUR 3-1 PALACE
Werner 77, Romero 80, Son 88
Eze 59

02/03/24: Spurs rebounded with some strength after an expert Eze free-kick had given the Eagles the lead at the Tottenham Hotspur Stadium. Glasner's first away game in charge of the side saw the record of Palace not beating Tottenham away since November 1997 remain.

BOURNEMOUTH 1-0 PALACE
Kluivert 79

02/04/24: With injuries taking their toll, Lerma moved into defence on a night to forget on the south coast for the Eagles after VAR had ruled out an early Eze goal.

PALACE 1-1 LUTON TOWN
Mateta 11,
Woodrow 90+6

09/03/24: Yet another late goal – this time with 96 minutes on the clock – saw Palace denied three points after Mateta's glorious back-heel flick had opened up the scoring.

PALACE 2-4 MANCHESTER CITY
Mateta 4, Édouard 86
De Bruyne 13, 70, Lewis 47, Haaland 66

06/04/24: Mateta scored early, but City bounced back in style, scoring four, unanswered goals. Édouard grabbed a consolation late on.

LIVERPOOL 0-1 PALACE
Eze 14

14/04/24: In what would later be voted Goal of the Season by the fans, Eze's simple finish by the six-yard box in front of the famous Kop, after a fantastic team move, was the difference between the two teams.

PALACE 2-0 NEWCASTLE UNITED
Mateta 55, 88

24/04/24: The Eagles – and Mateta in particular – kept soaring with a clear victory thanks to another two goals from the French striker, for the second time in four days.

PALACE 5-2 WEST HAM UNITED
Olise 7, Eze 16, Emerson 20 (og), Mateta 31, 64
Antonio 40, Henderson 89 (og)

21/04/24: The feelgood factor surrounding this game was palpable in the air. Beforehand fans were expectant of a performance and victory, but not one of them could have predicted seven goals – with five of them coming from the home side including Mateta again, this time with two.

FULHAM 1-1 PALACE
Muniz 52
Schlupp 87

27/04/24: A late contender for Goal of the Season saw Schlupp ensure a point for the Eagles against the West London outfit.

PALACE 4-0 MANCHESTER UNITED
Olise 12, 66, Mateta 40, Mitchell 58

06/05/24: United were taken apart in SE25 in a match which could have seen the visitors lose by even more. The result meant it was the first time in club history that the Eagles had completed the league double over United.

WOLVES 1-3 PALACE
Cunha 66
Olise 26, Mateta 28, Eze 73

11/05/24: The last away game of the season saw Olise and freshly-crowned Player of the Season, Mateta, score within 90 seconds of each other to put their side 2-0 up and cruising. It was Mateta's 10th goal in 11 games under Glasner.

PALACE 5-0 ASTON VILLA
Mateta 9, 39, 63, Eze 54, 69

19/05/24: A second set of five goals at Selhurst Park within four weeks secured a top-half finish, new record for top-flight league goals in a season (54) and joint-highest Premier League points tally (49).

It was apt that Mateta ended his season with a hat-trick, the first Palace league hat-trick since April 2015 as the home fans bid farewell to the long-serving James Tomkins and Jairo Riedewald who both came off of the bench late for their final Palace appearances after being released by the club.

The season ended with a lap of appreciation around the pitch, complete with speeches and awards in what would prove to be Michael Olise's last game for the club too, ahead of his move to Bayern Munich a few weeks later.

LEAGUE CUP

FA CUP

PLYMOUTH ARGYLE 2-4 PALACE
Waine 6, Cundle 46
Édouard 58, Mateta 61, 62, 83

29/08/23: Second Round: The Eagles came to life in the second half with three goals in four minutes as Mateta took the match ball home.

PALACE 0-0 EVERTON

04/01/24: Third Round: 2024 started with a scoreless draw in the FA Cup against Everton as França made his first start for the club.

MANCHESTER UNITED 3-0 PALACE
Garnacho 21, Casemiro 27, Martial 55

26/09/23: Third Round: Transfer window signings Dean Henderson and Rob Holding made their debuts, but it was one to forget for Henderson, playing against his former club, as he went off injured after just 19 minutes. Garnacho scored soon after and then Casemiro, to put the game to bed.

EVERTON 1-0 PALACE
Gomes 42

17/01/24: Third Round Replay: Palace were knocked out of the FA Cup, going down to a late first half strike from Andre Gomes.

WOMEN'S SEASON REVIEW 2023/24

In 2023/24, Crystal Palace Women made club history by winning the Barclays Championship title at Selhurst Park – and, with it, promotion to the top-flight for the very first time.

Pre-season saw a move to a new ground, the VBS Community Stadium in Sutton, a new Head Coach (Laura Kaminski), new Assistant Coach (Adam Jeffrey), new Head of Women's Football (Grace Williams) and eight new players.

After a strong set of pre-season results, Palace Women's first outing at Sutton, in August, saw a looping header in the 12th minute of additional time from Elise Hughes secure a point against Reading, just relegated from the Women's Super League.

In September a 2-1 win over Birmingham City at St Andrew's ignited Palace's season, swiftly followed by a 9-1 demolition of Durham in Sutton – a club-record win and later named the Performance of the Week by the League Managers' Association – before the side conceded a last-minute equaliser away to Sunderland. Annabel Blanchard claimed both the Championship's Player and Goal of the Month awards for September, with Kaminski taking Manager of the Month.

A 4-0 win over then-league leaders Blackburn Rovers at Ewood Park followed in October, with more goals the following week thanks to a 6-1 home win over London City Lionesses which saw the Eagles move up to third in the table. The month did see Palace suffer their first defeat of the season, a 2-3 loss, to Charlton at the Valley, despite Araya Dennis' Goal of the Season contender from 35 yards (which later won the league's monthly prize).

November would wipe away that disappointment, kicking off with 3-0 and 3-2 wins away to Watford and home to Lewes respectively. Then, the first attendance record fell: with Palace and Southampton battling at the top of the table, a club-record 4,442 fans at Selhurst Park witnessed a 4-3 thriller go in the Saints' favour.

Cup competitions took centre-stage in the winter months: a 3-0 win over Watford in the Continental League Cup group stages made up for the disappointment of a penalty shoot-out defeat to Lewes in the same competition. But both results were bettered by a thumping 6-0 win over Chatham Town in the Adobe Women's FA Cup third round, Hughes the provider of another hat-trick, and Sharpe with the pick of the goals.

With a 1-1 draw at Reading in December, Palace Women concluded 2023 in fourth place, just two points off the Championship summit.

Palace welcomed three fresh faces to South London in the January transfer window, with Ria Percival, Izzy Atkinson and Abbie Larkin all arriving. A dramatic 3-1 win over Blackburn in the FA Cup fourth-round – the first time Palace had won back-to-back games in the competition in their professional era – was followed by a hard-fought 2-0 win over London City Lionesses in the league, but a few days later Palace went out of the League Cup in the group stage after a 1-0 defeat to Charlton.

A superb 2-1 win over Southampton at St Mary's Stadium in the league followed in February as Izzy Atkinson grabbed her first goal for the club on the way to winning Championship Player of the Month. The Eagles then visited Emma Hayes' all-conquering Chelsea side in the FA Cup fifth-round with only a spectacular back-heeled finish in the 81st minute from Mayra Ramirez – the world's most expensive women's player – seeing the four-in-a-row Women's Super League champions progress at Palace's expense. They ended the month dispatching Blackburn in the league convincingly in Sutton as Kaminski was named Championship Manager of the Month for the second time.

March saw history made as the side won at Selhurst Park for the first time in the Championship against Sheffield United, with a scrappier return fixture a week later seeing the Blades claim revenge at Bramall Lane. Palace responded immediately with a 3-0 win over Watford, again at Selhurst Park – with another club-record 5,566 tickets sold and knowing that maximum points in the season run-in would secure promotion, a 5-1 win at Durham on Easter Sunday set Palace up perfectly for the final month.

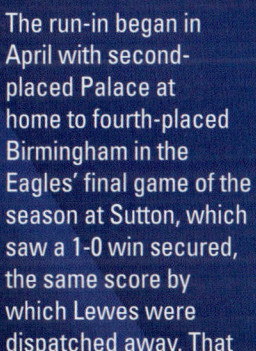

The run-in began in April with second-placed Palace at home to fourth-placed Birmingham in the Eagles' final game of the season at Sutton, which saw a 1-0 win secured, the same score by which Lewes were dispatched away. That result, in combination with Charlton's 1-0 win over Sunderland, meant that Palace were almost certain to win the Women's Championship title going into the final day, unless there was a remarkable three-point and 22-goal swing in the Addicks' favour.

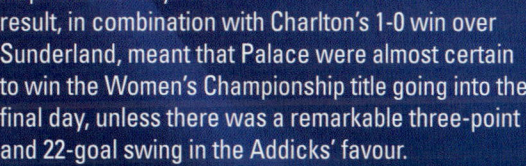

But it did not happen and in front of a record crowd of 6,796 at Selhurst Park, a 0-0 draw was enough to secure the trophy lift in SE25 – which you can see on the following pages.

BARCLAYS WOMEN'S CHAMPIONSHIP: CHAMPIONS 2023/24

"THIS CLUB IS VERY SPECIAL AND THE FANS ARE INVOLVED IN THAT. IT'S AN AMAZING ACHIEVEMENT. THERE'S LOTS TO LOOK FORWARD TO AND A LOT OF EXCITEMENT TO COME."

CAPTAIN AIMEE EVERETT

PREMIER LEAGUE INTERNATIONAL CUP: CHAMPIONS 2023/24

The Premier League International Cup is one of the leading European competitions in youth football, and the Eagles managed to win it in 2024, beating PSV Eindhoven after losing to them in the final in 2023.

GROUP STAGE

27/09/23	
Palace 1 - 1 Athletic Club	
Grehan 42	Duñabeitia 59

06/12/23	
Palace 2 - 1 SL Benfica	
Mathurin 10, Ola-Adebomi 87	Varela 59

24/10/23	
Palace 3 - 1 AS Monaco	
França 15, Ebiowei 33, Mathurin 87	Yacoub 83

17/01/24	
Palace 1 - 1 Feyenoord	
Plange 19	Hokke 14

> "WHAT A FEELING! WE PUT IN AN AMAZING PERFORMANCE AND WE'RE ABSOLUTELY BUZZING."
>
> **JOE WHITWORTH, GOALKEEPER AND CAPTAIN**

> "I SAID BEFORE THE GAME: IT'S ABOUT CREATING MEMORIES AND WHEREVER THESE PLAYERS GO IN THE GAME, YOU SHOULDN'T FORGET THESE MEMORIES. IT'S MASSIVE."
>
> **DARREN POWELL, UNDER-21S HEAD COACH**

QUARTER-FINAL
26/02/24
Palace 3 - 0 Wolves
Imray 15, 66
Mathurin 82

SEMI-FINAL
16/04/24
Palace 4 - 2 Everton
Umeh 45+3
Umolu 48   Metcalfe
Imray 70   63, 86
Devenny 90+3

FINAL
15/05/24
Palace 1 - 0 PSV Eindhoven
Umeh 67

RECORD BREAKERS
AND MILESTONES 2023/24 SEASON

PALACE MEN

Equal record Premier League finish:
10TH
(also in 2014/15)

Equal record highest Premier League points total: **49**
(achieved in 2018/19)

Record highest goals scored in Premier League season: **57**

FOUR
players in England squad for Euro 2024: Most from any club (Ebere Eze, Marc Guéhi, Dean Henderson and Adam Wharton)

Jean-Philippe Mateta became the first man since Yannick Bolasie in April 2015 to score a Premier League hat-trick for the club – a first-ever home Premier League hat-trick in Palace's history

Mateta scored in seven, consecutive top-flight home matches – a Palace record.

10X3
First time in Palace's top-flight history that three players (Mateta 16, Eze 11 and Olise 10) have all scored 10 or more goals in the same season.

Four straight home wins for the first time in the Premier League (and for the first time since 1990/91)

PALACE WOMEN

Record points tally: **46**

Record goals scored in the Championship (club record): **55**

Record club attendance (at Selhurst Park vs Sunderland): **6,796**

Record attendance at Sutton (vs Charlton) **989**

Championship Most Assists: **8** Fliss Gibbons

Championship Golden Boot: Elise Hughes

16 GOALS

Biggest Championship win:
9–1
vs Durham
(league and club record)

LMA Manager of the Season: Laura Kaminski

AWARD WINNERS

The 2023/24 Crystal Palace FC Awards took place in front of hundreds of fans at the Fairfield Halls in Croydon, South London.

MEN'S PLAYER OF THE SEASON
JEAN-PHILIPPE MATETA

WOMEN'S PLAYER OF THE SEASON
ELISE HUGHES

MEN'S PLAYERS' PLAYER OF THE SEASON
JEAN-PHILIPPE MATETA & JOACHIM ANDERSEN

WOMEN'S PLAYERS' PLAYER OF THE SEASON
SHANADE HOPCROFT

GOAL OF THE SEASON
EBERE EZE V LIVERPOOL (A) – 14 APRIL 2024

MOMENT OF THE SEASON
PALACE WOMEN SECURING PROMOTION AND BREAKING THEIR ATTENDANCE RECORD

UNDER-21 MEN'S PLAYER OF THE SEASON
JOE WHITWORTH

UNDER-18 MEN'S PLAYER OF THE SEASON
JESSE DERRY

PFA COMMUNITY CHAMPIONS
AIMEE EVERETT & CHRIS RICHARDS

CHAIRMAN'S AWARD FOR OUTSTANDING CONTRIBUTION
JOEL WARD

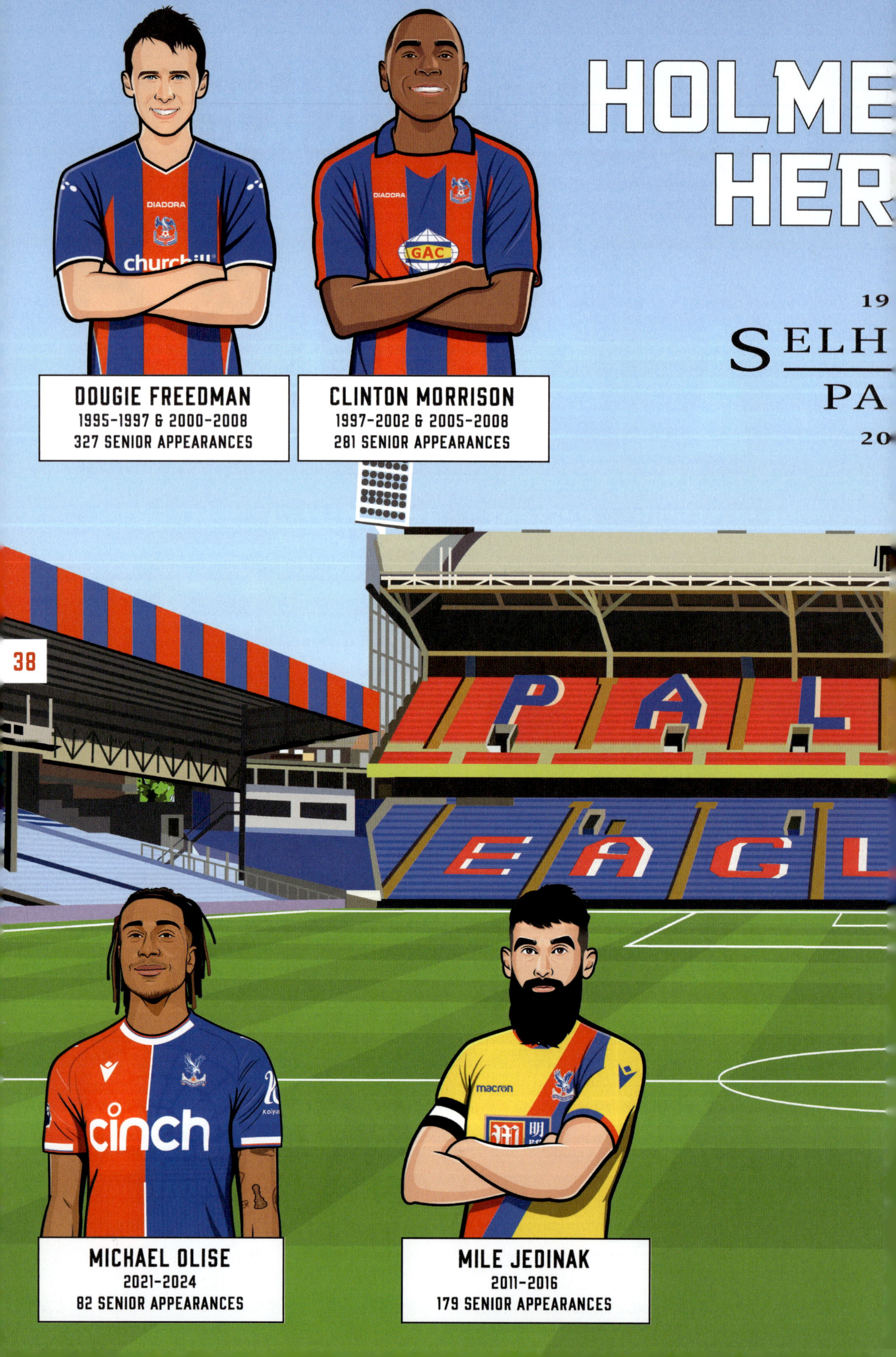

DOUGIE FREEDMAN
1995-1997 & 2000-2008
327 SENIOR APPEARANCES

CLINTON MORRISON
1997-2002 & 2005-2008
281 SENIOR APPEARANCES

MICHAEL OLISE
2021-2024
82 SENIOR APPEARANCES

MILE JEDINAK
2011-2016
179 SENIOR APPEARANCES

SDALE
OES

4
URST
RK
24

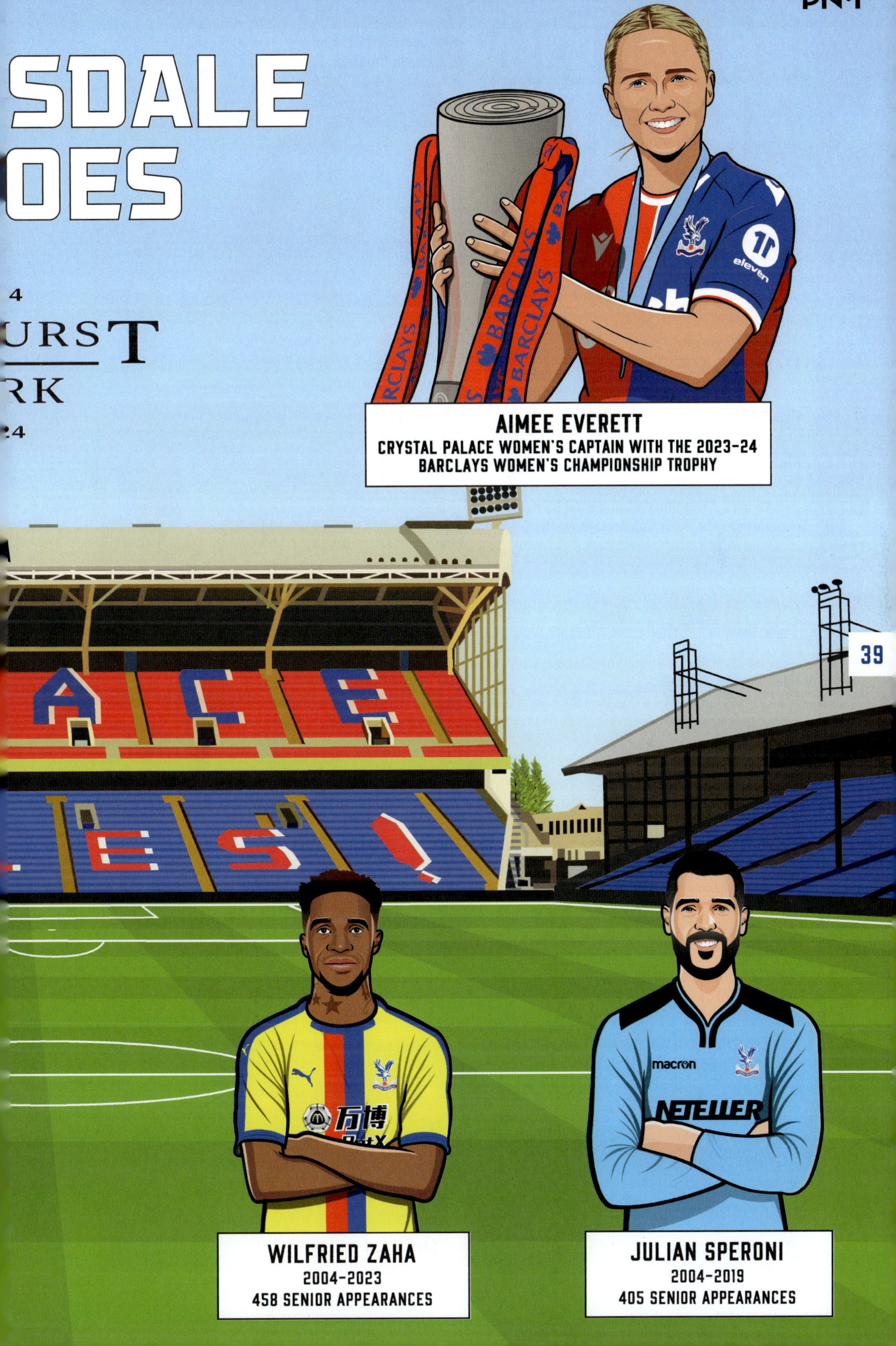

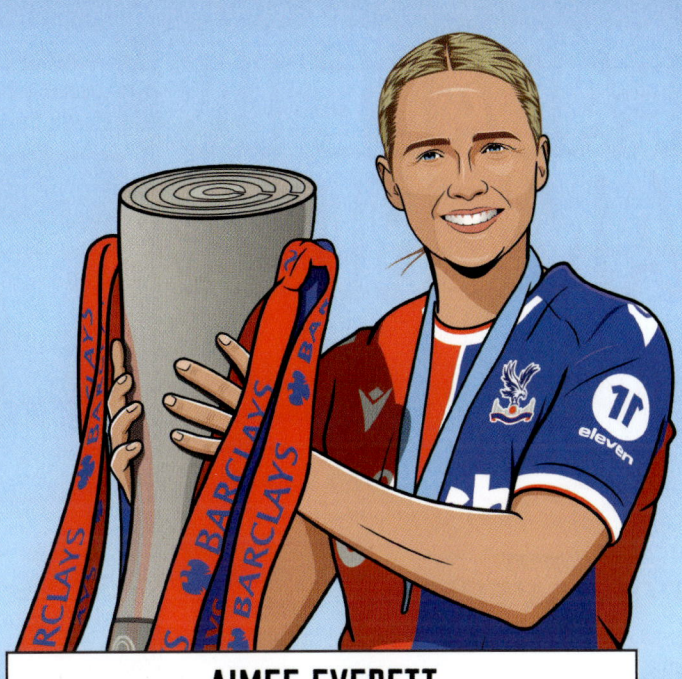

AIMEE EVERETT
CRYSTAL PALACE WOMEN'S CAPTAIN WITH THE 2023-24 BARCLAYS WOMEN'S CHAMPIONSHIP TROPHY

WILFRIED ZAHA
2004-2023
458 SENIOR APPEARANCES

JULIAN SPERONI
2004-2019
405 SENIOR APPEARANCES

PALACE IN AMERICA

CONMEBOL COPA AMERICA USA 2024

The summer of 2024 saw Palace players involved with Colombia and the United States of America at the CONMEBOL Copa América held in the USA.

Defender Chris Richards represented the United States – coached by former Palace player Gregg Berhalter – while fellow defender Daniel Muñoz and midfielder Jefferson Lerma represented Colombia. Both teams met in a friendly before the competition too, with Colombia winning 5-1.

COLOMBIA 🇨🇴

Monday 24 June: Preliminary Group D
Colombia 2-1 Paraguay
NRG Stadium, Houston

Friday 28 June: Preliminary Group D
Colombia 3-0 Costa Rica
State Farm Stadium, Glendale, Arizona

Tuesday 2 July: Preliminary Group D
Brazil 1-1 Colombia
Levi's Stadium, Santa Clara, California

Saturday 6 July: Quarter-Final
Colombia 5-0 Panama
State Farm Stadium, Glendale, Arizona

Wednesday 10 July: Semi-Final
Uruguay 0-1 Colombia
Bank of America Stadium, Charlotte, North Carolina

Sunday 14 July 14: Final
Argentina 1-0 Colombia (aet)
Hard Rock Stadium, Miami Gardens

UNITED STATES OF AMERICA

Sunday 23 June: Preliminary Group D
United States 2-0 Bolivia
AT&T Stadium, Arlington

Thursday 27 June: Preliminary Group D
Panama 2-1 United States
Mercedes-Benz Stadium, Atlanta

Monday 1 July
United States 0-1 Uruguay
Arrowhead Stadium, Kansas City

PALACE TOUR TO THE USA

Last July and August the Men's first-team squad travelled to the east coast of the USA to play in a pre-season tournament.

The Eagles beat Wolves 3-1 at the ground of former club franchise Crystal Palace USA – the Navy-Marine Corps Memorial Stadium in Maryland and a few days later at the Raymond James Stadium in Tampa, they won by the same score against West Ham to lift the Stateside Cup.

In addition to the games, there was open training in Baltimore and Tampa, a visit to a Baltimore Orioles baseball game and a Washington D.C. tour including the White House.

Plenty of Eagles fans were present, many of whom are part of official fan clubs out in the USA.

Crystal Palace have supporters' clubs all around the world, for more information, visit: www.cpfc.co.uk/supporters/supporting-overseas

FORWARDS

JEAN-PHILIPPE MATETA

ELISE HUGHES

ISMAÏLA SARR

WORDFIT

Can you fit these 25 past Palace Men's and Women's Player of the Year award winners into the grid?

4 LETTERS
AYEW
CORT
DANN

5 LETTERS
BOYCE
BRYAN
CLYNE

6 LETTERS
BARRON
BRIGHT
CANNON
GUAITA
HINCKS
HOPKIN
HUGHES

7 LETTERS
COLEMAN
EVERETT
GILBERT
JEDINAK

8 LETTERS
BAPTISTE
DOUCOURÉ
EDWORTHY
FREEDMAN
HOLDAWAY
JEFFRIES

9 LETTERS
GALLAGHER

11 LETTERS
HINSHELWOOD

Solution on Page 61!

2024 EUROPEAN CHAMPIONSHIP

The summer of 2024 saw Palace players involved in both the Paris 2024 Olympic Games and 2024 UEFA Men's European Championship in Germany.

Euro 2024 saw five Crystal Palace players represent their countries. Four Eagles were in the Three Lions – with Ebere Eze, Marc Guéhi, Dean Henderson and Adam Wharton all selected by former Palace defender Gareth Southgate for his England squad which made it all the way to the final!

It was the first time in history that four Crystal Palace players were selected for a senior England squad at an international competition.

Also, former Palace defender Joachim Andersen was selected for Denmark and even played against his SE25 central defensive partner Marc Guéhi!

ENGLAND

Sunday 16 June: Preliminary Group C
Serbia 0-1 England
Arena AufSchalke, Gelsenkirchen

England opened their campaign with a win thanks to a Jude Bellingham goal in the 13th minute.

Guéhi – played whole match
Eze, Henderson, Wharton – unused substitutes

Thursday 20 June: Preliminary Group C
Denmark 1-1 England
Frankfurt Arena, Frankfurt am Main

A Harry Kane 18th-minute strike was cancelled out by a rocket from Denmark's Morten Hjulmand 17 minutes later. The game saw Palace players on both sides with Guéhi and Eze going up against Andersen.

Guéhi – played whole match
Eze – came on as 70th-minute substitute
Henderson, Wharton – unused substitutes

Tuesday 25 June: Preliminary Group C
England 0-0 Slovenia
Cologne Stadium, Cologne

The stalemate sees England win their group to progress through to the Round of 16.

Guéhi – played whole match
Eze, Henderson, Wharton – unused substitutes

Sunday 30 June: Round of 16
England 2-1 Slovakia (aet)
Arena AufSchalke, Gelsenkirchen

After Ivan Schranz had put the underdogs Slovakia ahead in the first half, a spectacular bicycle kick from Jude Bellingham in the fifth minute of additional time took the game to extra time. Harry Kane's header in the first minute of the extra period saw the Three Lions through to the last eight. Eze and Guéhi were involved with both England goals.

Guéhi – played whole match
Eze – came on as 84th-minute substitute
Henderson, Wharton – unused substitutes

Saturday 6 July: Quarter-Final
England 1-1 Switzerland
(England win 5-3 on penalties)
Düsseldorf Arena, Düsseldorf

With Guéhi suspended due to his yellow card against Slovakia, the sole Palace representation was Eze, who came on with his side 1-0 down after a Breel Embolo shot in the 75th minute. However, within two minutes of coming on, Eze and England had drawn level thanks to Bukayo Sako. His goal took the game to extra time, then penalties, with Trent Alexander-Arnold scoring the winning one after Manuel Akanji had missed.

Eze – came on as 78th minute substitute
Guéhi – missed game due to suspension
Henderson, Wharton – unused substitutes

Wednesday 10 July: Semi-Final
Netherlands 1-2 England
BVB Stadion Dortmund, Dortmund

A second, successive European Championship semi-final saw England go behind again, with Xavi Simons' strike in the seventh minute, but a VAR-given Harry Kane penalty 10 minutes later brought the teams equal. Substitute Ollie Watkins then scored a spectacular winner in the 90th minute – with the striker running over to celebrate with substitutes including Henderson and Wharton.

Guéhi – played whole match
Eze, Henderson, Wharton – unused substitutes

Sunday 14 July: Final
Spain 2-1 England - Olympiastadion, Berlin

After losing the 2020 Euro final to Italy on penalties, England were determined to win the 2024 edition, but it was not to be as a superior Spain went ahead shortly into the second half thanks to Nico Williams. A Cole Palmer strike made it all-square with just over 15 minutes left, but Mikel Oyarzabal had other ideas, his close-range strike sealing the title with just four minutes remaining despite a late headed chance from Guéhi which was cleared off of the line.

Guéhi – played whole match
Eze, Henderson, Wharton – unused substitutes

Following the conclusion of the tournament, Guéhi was named in the Opta Team of the Tournament and awarded a special EA FC 24 Ultimate Team card.

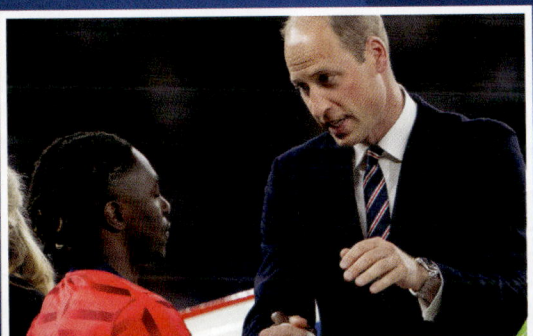

JOACHIM ANDERSEN

Former Palace man Joachim Andersen played every minute of all four of Denmark's games which saw them make the Round of 16, where they lost to the host nation Germany. In an eventful game, which was partly suspended due to thunderstorms, Andersen thought he had put the Danes ahead with his first international goal, but it was ruled out for offside after a lengthy and controversial VAR check.

And just minutes later, VAR went against Andersen again, with technology inside the ball determining a handball from the Palace defender in the area. Kai Havertz sunk home the penalty for Germany to make it 1-0 in the 53rd minute and a Jamal Musiala strike 15 minutes later, put the hosts through and the Danes out.

Sunday 16 June: Preliminary Group C
Slovenia 1-1 Denmark
Stuttgart Arena, Stuttgart

Thursday 20 June: Preliminary Group C
Denmark 1-1 England
Frankfurt Arena, Frankfurt am Main

Tuesday 25 June: Preliminary Group C
Denmark 0-0 Serbia
Munich Football Arena, Munich

Saturday 29 June: Round of 16
Germany 2-0 Denmark
BVB Stadion Dortmund, Dortmund

MATETA IN PARIS

Eagles' striker Jean-Philippe Mateta and midfielder, Michael Olise – before his move to Bayern Munich – were named by Thierry Henry to be part of the France men's Olympic Games team for the Paris 2024 Olympic Games.

And what a Games it was for them! France made it all the way to the final, winning silver with Mateta becoming the first-ever Crystal Palace player (for either the 1861 amateur or 1905 professional outfits) to win an Olympic medal while playing for the club.

Wednesday 24 July - Preliminary Group A
France 3-0 United States of America
Marseille Stadium, Marseille

Mateta played 71 minutes before being subbed off as former Palace player Olise scored in a comprehensive opening win for the host nation.

Friday 2 August - Quarter-Fina
France 1-0 Argentina
Marseille Stadium, Marseille

A fiery encounter saw Mateta's fifth minute header confirm France's place in the semi-finals. He played the whole 90 minutes.

Saturday 27 July - Preliminary Group A
France 1-0 Guinea
Nice Stadium, Nice

A goal from Kiliann Sildillia was enough to make it two from two as Mateta played 58 minutes before being substituted.

Monday 5 August - Semi-Final
France 3-1 Egypt (aet)
Lyon Stadium, Lyon

An 83rd minute equaliser from Mateta took the game to extra time and he then put his side ahead in the 99th minute, the 3-1 victory sealed by Olise. Mateta was subbed off with two minutes remaining.

Tuesday 30 July - Preliminary Group A
New Zealand 0-3 France
Marseille Stadium, Marseille

A goal from captain Mateta in the 19th minute paved the way for a third win in three for France as the Palace striker was subbed off in the 66th minute.

Friday 9 August - Gold Medal Match
France 3-5 Spain (aet)
Parc des Princes, Paris

An all-time classic saw a 90+3 penalty from Mateta take the game to extra time, with the hosts left heartbroken thanks to a brace from Spain's substitute, Sergio Camello.

HISTORY MAKERS

ANNABEL JOHNSON
Defender
2018-2024
All-time appearance maker (professional era) for Palace women: 86

JIM CANNON
Defender
1973-1988
Most senior appearances: 660

EDMUND GOODMAN
1907-1925
Longest serving manager: 18 years

ANDREW JOHNSON
2002-2006 & 2014-2015
Most league goals in a top-flight season: 21 (2004/05)

CHRISTIAN BENTEKE
2016-2022
Highest international goalscorer while at club: 11 goals for Belgium

MARC GUÉHI
2021-Present
First player to start in international final for England while at club – Euro 2024, v Spain (14/07/2024)

GREGG BERHALTER
2001-2002
First Crystal Palace player to appear in a FIFA World Cup – for USA v Mexico (17/06/2002)

SPOT THE BALL

The ball has disappeared! Can you spot where it should be?

SPOT THE DIFFERENCE

Can you spot the 10 differences between these two photos?

Answers on Page 61!

We are Palace for Life, the official charity of Crystal Palace FC. We have been a core part of the south London community for over 25 years. Football is more than just a game, it is also about community and that is what we are all about.

Most of our work is around offering free, accessible football activities in south London, but we also help people find a job or support them in other ways through mentoring. Here are some of the things we did last season!

MEETING THE PALACE SQUADS AT THE ACADEMY

The Crystal Palace Men's and Women's first team squads and coaching staff came to the Academy to experience the work we do with young people all year-round.

The players experienced a twist on one-to-one mentoring, where our participants delivered a session with them, they took penalties with our famous DS Eagles, brushed up on their maths skills and were challenged by our Get Involved, Premier League Kicks, and Girls Emerging Talent Centre participants.

The visit was even shown on Match of the Day!

THOUSANDS RAISED IN 'BIKE TO WOLVES' AND 'MARATHON MARCH' CHALLENGES

Over 100 Palace fans took on our annual charity fundraiser, the 'Marathon March', walking 26.2 miles around south London to raise money for our programmes. Together, they raised over £100,000 – incredible!

And in our 'Bike to Wolves' challenge, 34 cyclists rode from Selhurst Park all the way to the Wolverhampton Wanderers' stadium – a huge 160 miles – and raised £48,000!

NATHANIEL CLYNE UNVEILS OUR LIMITED EDITION FOURTH SHIRT

Crystal Palace defender, former academy player and south Londoner himself Nathaniel Clyne visited his old school to unveil our limited edition fourth shirt. Only 1,000 were available and they sold out in a matter of days. All proceeds from the shirts went straight towards our work.

GUÉHI JOINS IN WITH PREMIER LEAGUE KICKS

Marc Guéhi coached four of our most talented players who come to our weekly Premier League Kicks football sessions.

PALACE AID

We hosted over 40 celebrities, comedians, rappers, YouTubers and former footballers to take part in our biggest charity football match ever at Selhurst Park, raising lots of funds in the process.

JOHNSTONE GOES BACK TO SCHOOL FOR WORLD BOOK DAY

Goalkeeper Sam Johnstone went back to school to talk all about World Book Day at an assembly in a school in Bromley.

HOW MENTORING HELPED MARY ACHIEVE HER GREEN DREAMS

17-year-old Mary's struggles with anxiety left her feeling uncertain about her future, but she was certain that she wanted to pursue her dream of working in sustainability and politics. With the help of our mentoring and employment team, Mary was quickly snapped up for an apprenticeship in sustainability and is well on the way to achieving her green dreams.

Her mentor said: "It's been incredible to watch Mary's confidence and resilience grow as she's progressed through the programme. She's shown real determination and a willingness to confront her challenges. She's worked incredibly hard and should be extremely proud of her achievements."

Find out more and get involved through participating in sessions, volunteering, fundraising and lots more by following us: @PalaceForLife

@PalaceForLife

100 YEARS OF SELHURST PARK

On 30 August 2024 Selhurst Park – the home of Crystal Palace FC – celebrated its 100th Anniversary. Using the club archive and historian Ian King, plus the magic Lego constructions of Palace fan Chris from Brickstand, we take a look at key events at the stadium from the past 100 years…

SELHURST PARK
1924 — 2024

FEBRUARY 1919
The club lease a 15-acre piece of wasteland at Selhurst which had once been a brickfield and had two chimney stacks standing.

JANUARY 1922
£2,570 was paid by an agent, Mr. Richardson, for the freehold of the ground.

AUGUST 1924
Crystal Palace move up the road from 'The Nest' at Selhurst station to their new ground, 'Selhurst Park'. After spending £30,000 on getting the site ready, with its solitary stand, the 'Main Stand', nearly finished, it is ready to open.

In front of a crowd estimated to be between 20-25,000, Palace play their first game at their new home, losing 1-0 to 'The Wednesday', now called Sheffield Wednesday.

MARCH 1926
The only England match to date at Selhurst Park saw the national team take on Wales, who won 3-1 in the 'Home International Clash' on St. David's Day.

APRIL 1962
Real Madrid came to SE25 to play Palace in a friendly match in front of 25,000 fans to celebrate the installation of new floodlights – which had been installed in 1961 featuring four pylons. The crowd witnessed the delights of Alfredo Di Stéfano and Ferenc Puskás.

SUMMER 1935
New scoreboards are installed and the ditch at the side of the pitch filled in. A water tap was also installed next to the dug-outs for the sponge and bucket of water!

JULY-AUGUST 1948
The 1948 Olympic Games were held in London with Selhurst Park hosting two football matches – Denmark beating Egypt 3-1 (aet) on 31 July in their first round clash, and eventual gold medallists Sweden beating South Korea 12-0 a few days later in their quarter-final on 5 August.

SUMMER 1965
The dressing rooms were refurbished with a new lounge, games room and tea room for the players under the Main Stand. The 'Glaziers Club' was enlarged too.

AUGUST 1967
A new club office block opened at the back of the Main Stand with a new Boardroom, offices and reception area.

OCTOBER 1968
Work commences on the new 'Arthur Wait' stand.

SUMMER 1969
The Whitehorse Lane end saw a 'second tier' of terracing constructed, complete with brick-built refreshments and toilets at the top. A new Supporters Club was built in the car park.

NOVEMBER 1969
A second stand is opened – the Arthur Wait stand, named after the Palace chairman and featuring 5,032 seats with space in front for 8,000 standing. It is opened officially with the playing of the 'Arthur Rowe Testimonial Match' with Palace taking on an 'International XI'. The season would end with the club promoted to the top-flight for the first time.

SUMMER 1953
Basic floodlights are installed, strung along Park Road and on the Main Stand roof.

DECEMBER 1972
Palace beat Manchester United 5-0 thanks to goals from Mulligan, Rogers and Whittle.

MAY 1979
A record 51,482 supporters cram into Selhurst Park to see Palace beat Burnley 2-0 to celebrate promotion to the top-flight.

SUMMER 1980
The Main Stand enclosure for standing is converted to seating, and the Whitehorse Lane end is demolished for Sainsbury's. New barriers, fencing and sectioning are completed in the Holmesdale End.

SUMMER 1981
Executive Boxes are added to the Main Stand.

JULY 1983
Peter Gabriel, Thompson Twins and Undertones play a music concert on the Selhurst Park pitch.

JULY 1984
The 'Reggae Sunsplash', featuring Prince Buster, The Skatelites, Sly and Robbie, Black Uhuru, King Sunny Ade, Lloyd Parkes and We People, Leroy Sibbles, Dennis Brown and Aswad takes place in SE25 – the success is repeated the following year.

SEPTEMBER 1985
Local rivals Charlton Athletic become tenants at Selhurst Park after getting into financial troubles. They would be based in SE25 until 1991.

JUNE 1989
The Eagles celebrate promotion to the top flight with a play-off second leg win over Blackburn Rovers.

SUMMER 1990
The Main Stand dressing rooms and players exit onto pitch are moved to the Holmesdale Road, a new Player's Lounge is built and the main reception area is extended. The Arthur Wait standing enclosure is converted to seating.

JUNE 1991
Selhurst Park welcomes its second groundshare team, Wimbledon, who move from Plough Lane due to financial issues, before leaving in 2003.

SUMMER 1991
Whitehorse Lane Executive Boxes are built.

AUGUST 1992
The first-ever Premier League game takes place at Selhurst Park, with Mark Bright opening the scoring in a 3-3 draw with Blackburn Rovers, featuring Alan Shearer scoring his first Premier League goal.

SUMMER 1993
The Whitehorse Lane standing enclosure is converted into seating.

MAY 1994

Palace captain Gareth Southgate lifts the First Division trophy as the Eagles are crowned champions and gain promotion back to the Premier League as the Holmesdale Road terrace closes for the last time ahead of the new stand development.

SUMMER 1994

The Whitehorse Lane end roof is erected with a Philips Al Fresco video screen.

1995

Construction is in full swing of the new Holmesdale Road stand.

SEPTEMBER 1995

The new Holmesdale Road, two-tiered, all-seater stand opens.

OCTOBER 2002

The Eagles beat Brighton 5-0 thanks to an Andy Johnson hat-trick as legendary Crystal Palace manager Steve Coppell returns to Selhurst Park, but this time as the away team manager.

JUNE 2010

Four businessmen and Palace fans - Steve Parish, Stephen Browett, Martin Long and Jeremy Hosking - form the 'CPFC 2010' consortium and save the club from bankruptcy.

2023

Preparatory work starts on the planned, new Main Stand.

APRIL 2024

In front of a record crowd for the team of 6,796, Palace Women clinch the FA Women's Championship title with a draw against Sunderland to gain promotion to the Women's Super League (WSL) for the first time in their history.

JUNE 2024

Crystal Palace fan Richard Riakporhe takes on Chris Billam-Smith for the WBO cruiserweight boxing title at Selhurst Park.

Follow Chris and Brickstand: Twitter @brickstand Instagram @fcbrickstand

COLOUR IN

Pete and Alice the Eagle are the Official Crystal Palace F.C. Mascots who have been keeping fans of all ages entertained at Selhurst Park for many years. Pete wears Number 18 on his back and Alice Number 61. Together they are '1861' – the year the amateur club was founded.

Give them some colour and why not colour in the club crest too…

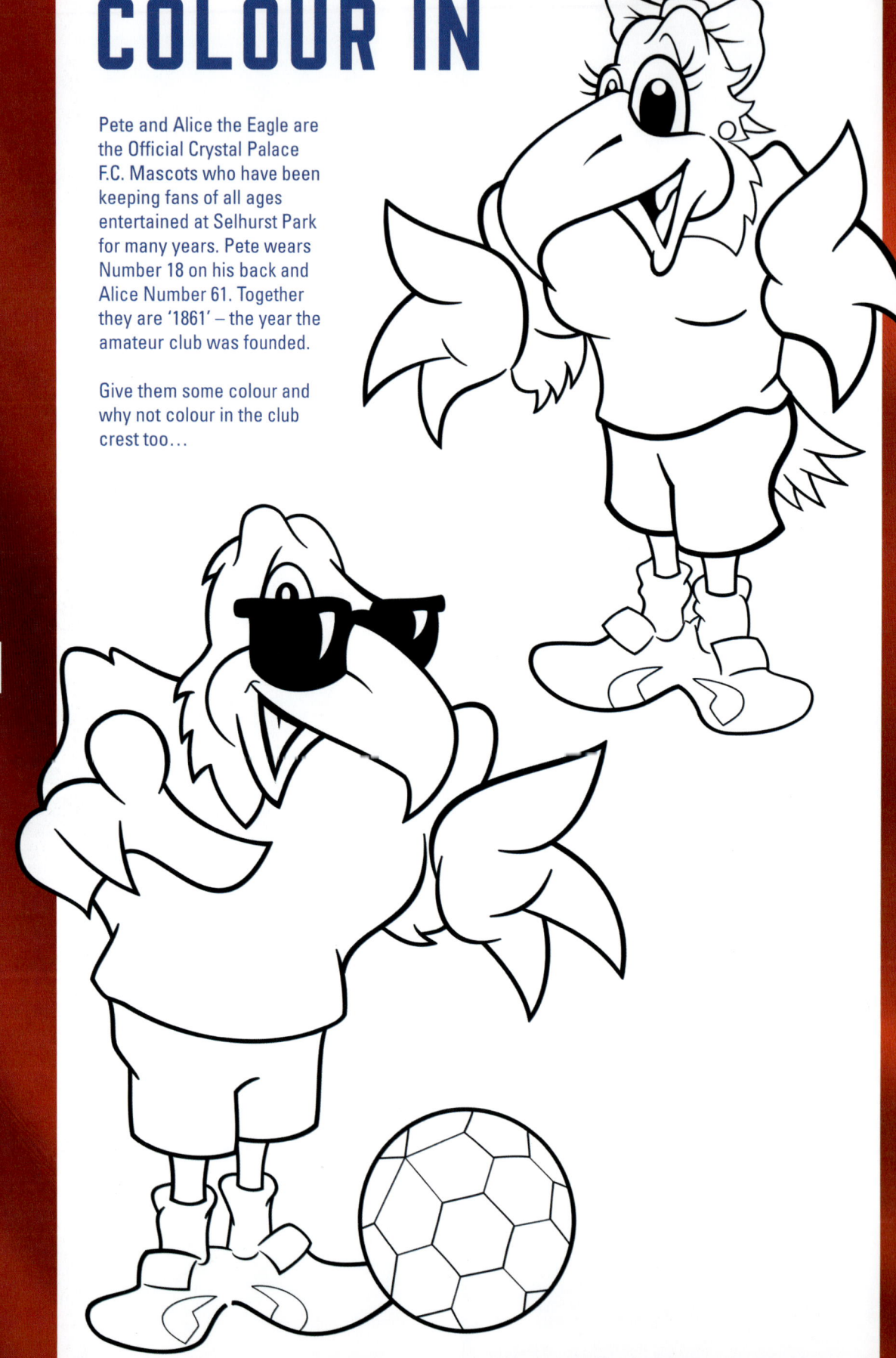

ANSWERS

P43 WORD FIT

(crossword solution with answers: boyce, jedinak, everett, baptiste, bright, freedman, insher, gallagher, baron, cort, clyne, coleman, jeffries, holdaway, ducoure, hinks, gilbert, edworthy, hughes, guaita, hopkins, cannon, bryan, dann)

P50 SPOT THE BALL

ANSWER: A

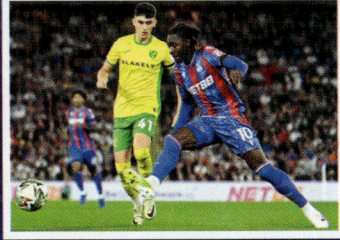

ANSWER: E

P51 SPOT THE DIFFERENCE

Feeling 'Glad All Over' you got the answers right?

Why not learn the words to the famous chant you have heard being sung during Palace games? It is called 'Glad All Over' and when the team made the FA Cup Final in 1990 they even recorded their own version.

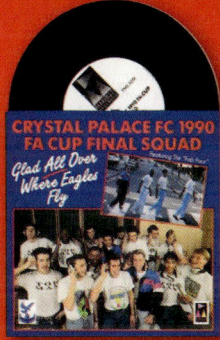

GLAD ALL OVER – THE LYRICS

Verse

You say that you love me
(Say you love me)
All of the time
(All of the time)
You say that you need me
(Say you need me)
You'll always be mine
(Always be mine)

Chorus

And I'm feelin'…Glad All Over
Yes, I'm…Glad All Over
Baby, I'm…Glad All Over
So glad you're mine…….

Verse

I'll make you happy
(Make you happy)
You'll never be blue
(Never be blue)
You'll have no sorrow
(Have no sorrow)
'Cause I'll always be true
(Always be true)
[repeat chorus]

Verse

Other girls may try to take me away (Take me away)
But you know, it's by your side I will stay
I'll stay
Our love will last now
(Our love will last)
'Til the end of time
(End of time)
Because this love now
(Because this love)
Is only yours and mine
(Yours and mine)
[repeat chorus]

61